Original title:
The Corner of the Room

Copyright © 2025 Creative Arts Management OÜ
All rights reserved.

Author: Rory Fitzgerald
ISBN HARDBACK: 978-1-80587-062-3
ISBN PAPERBACK: 978-1-80587-532-1

Remnants of the Past

Dust bunnies dance in a gleeful spree,
Forgotten socks with a sense of glee.
Chairs hold secrets, tales unreal,
Of stumbles and tumbles, what's the deal?

A teacup chipped, it grins so wide,
Filling with stories, it cannot hide.
Mismatched items make quite a crew,
In their own world, they have much to do.

Spaces Where Dreams Collide

The vacuum hums a lullaby tune,
While an old clock winks at the moon.
Papers flutter with secrets untold,
In this playful realm, they're bold and old.

A cat naps soundly on a stack of books,
Dreaming of mice with curious looks.
Clouds of laughter fill the air with glee,
As shadows join in this wild jubilee.

Silent Layers of Being

Beneath the layers of forgotten threads,
Yellowed papers and dust-covered beds.
Whispers of laughter linger in space,
Where odd objects share a warm embrace.

A rug with stains, each a comical tale,
Of spilled drinks and snacks, oh, how they sail!
Bounding through time, they put on a show,
In this quirky land, happiness flows.

The Invisible Embrace

Socks sneak away, on mischief they thrive,
In a world where giggles come alive.
Curtains shiver with a knowing smile,
As adventures unfold with each passing mile.

Plants eavesdrop on stories untold,
In this vibrant space, they're never cold.
With sprinkles of joy and just a touch of woe,
Life's little mishaps steal the show.

Forgotten Corners of the Mind

In a shadowy space, where thoughts like dust bunnies roam,
A lost sock and a sandwich, create a cozy home.
There sits my old diary, with secrets gone stale,
Pondering the day when I chased my dream's tail.

A jigsaw puzzle missing, the piece shaped like cheese,
Laughter echoes softly, causing my mind to tease.
Where did I put laughter? Ah, hidden under stacks,
Of half-eaten cookies, and my love for snacks.

Frayed Edges of an Old Dream

Once a castle was built, in blueprints no one saw,
Populated by giggles and a life full of awe.
Now it's more of a lean-to, with a roof full of holes,
And a moat made of juice boxes, guarding snack time goals.

Some dreams fray at the edges, like an old pair of socks,
Hiding their glory beneath tangled thoughts in boxes.
But still, I find treasures in the frays and seams,
Like laughter wrapped in whispers of whimsical dreams.

Reflections in a Cracked Mirror

Oh look at that fellow, with hair like a mop,
A silly old figure, in my favorite shop.
The mirror's a joker, it bends and it dips,
Yet it surely won't stop me from making my quips.

Each crack a reminder of laughter and tears,
Reflecting my antics across the long years.
What stories you tell, my dear glassy friend,
Of shenanigans past and the laughter that won't end.

Stillness Breathing in the Dark

In the still of the night, when my thoughts often creep,
I hear the tick-tock, and a snooze from the heap.
Monsters take sips of their juice in delight,
While shadows trade jokes in the absence of light.

Whispers wander softly, dressed in starlit attire,
Telling silly stories, igniting my fire.
Even in darkness, the chuckles arise,
And maybe just maybe, the world's full of pies.

Unraveled Threads of Yesterday

In the nook where dust bunnies play,
I found missing socks and a tray.
An old shoe, a half-eaten snack,
Who said this space is a lack?

A forgotten toy, a jumbled mix,
Puzzle pieces, family tricks.
Laughter echoes, sweet and proud,
As I juggle the chaos aloud.

Fleeting Moments

Right by the wall, a coat's new home,
Where secrets hide and whispers roam.
A paperweight turned into a friend,
In this mess, the stories blend.

Tangled hair ties, a cat's delight,
A dance of shadows, oh what a sight!
Tickling my nose, a breeze with flair,
Why did I think no one would care?

Permanent Marks

In this hub of ink spills and doodles,
Sketchbook dreams and forgotten poodles.
Fingers smudged, a toast to fate,
On the wall, my artwork's first date.

With crayons bright, I made my stand,
Here's to spills and choices unplanned.
The paint may chip, the scribbles stay,
A masterpiece of a messy day.

Beneath the Surface of Solitude

In the quiet hush, a sock takes flight,
Waltzing with dust in the soft moonlight.
An unclaimed sandwich, it's quite a find,
In this little hub, all are entwined.

Whispers giggle from shadows ahead,
Jokes shared with crumbs of old bread.
Who knew silence could spark such glee?
In this cozy chaos, we tease destiny.

A Sanctuary for Lost Voices

Here lies a haven for wishes unspoken,
Jokes caught in laughter, none left broken.
A broken clock and mismatched shoes,
Tales of mischief, a friend to choose.

Amid vibrant chaos and playful charms,
I host conversations with invisible arms.
The air is thick with joy's embrace,
In this quirky spot, we've found our place.

Solitary Epiphanies

In shadows, I ponder, what is real?
A sock has vanished, what a steal!
A plant gives whispers, oh so sly,
It knows my secrets, without a why.

Dust bunnies dance, caught in the light,
I swear they giggle, oh what a sight!
My thoughts collide, bump like a bee,
In this quiet chaos, just me and me.

The Imprint of Presence

A mug sits idle, half full of tea,
It's cold now, like my social glee.
Each chair a witness, to my grand show,
Where did I put that last piece, though?

Lonely socks gossip, I hear their tales,
Imaginary friends, oh how it pales!
Curious shadows come out to play,
In my absent-minded, one-man ballet.

Gatherings of Lost Time

A spoon sings softly, what a delight,
While forks roll their eyes in the dim light.
I wave at the clock, stuck in a loop,
Time's just a prankster, a fickle group.

Old postcards giggle, of journeys past,
I muse at my travel, all too vast.
My cat, unimpressed, yawns with a sigh,
I guess even felines love to fly.

The Muffled Heartbeat

Naps on the couch, the best kinda bliss,
While dust motes dance, oh what have I missed?
The fridge hums a tune, just like my dreams,
In this crowded silence, nothing's as it seems.

Empty bags whisper, a feast had once,
Crumbs tell tales, of culinary dunce.
A chair creaks loudly, a joke just for me,
In this odd little realm, I'm forever free.

Overlooked Paths of Reflection

In the shadow, dust bunnies play,
Whiskers twitching, they dance all day.
Socks lost in the legendary fight,
A plush unicorn takes its flight.

Mismatched slippers form a parade,
While crumbs and secrets serenade.
Behind the chair, a snack remains,
Oh, how the curtain tightly strains!

Puddles of cocoa spill their dreams,
Not all is quiet, or so it seems.
A chair relinquishes its stare,
What wonders hide in the worn-out air?

Echoes of laughter long forgiven,
Dust motes twirl—would they be driven?
A hidden joy in every nook,
If only the world would take a look.

Nuances of Untold Stories

Beneath the table, a sock's lament,
Its partner's gone; time's discontent.
A paperclip holds secrets tight,
In a game of hide and seek at night.

The shelf speaks volumes, but who will hear?
A dusty book sheds a connoisseur's tear.
From furry cushions, sighs arise,
"Why must we be so hard to find?"

A coffee cup's whispers linger still,
Sharing tales with thrifted quill.
Behind a curtain, a fleeting glance,
Socks and spoons waltz in a trance.

Silent witnesses of a glorious mess,
Spilled laughter and a touch of distress.
Each object has danced, each dust moted leaf,
Hiding stories beyond belief.

Dimensions of Stillness

In the stillness, a tangle of chairs,
Collecting whispers that float in airs.
A haughty plant in a plastic cage,
Gives side-eye to the old, worn stage.

The clock ticks loudly, a comic relief,
Time rebels against its own brief.
A moth takes cover in careless glee,
While dust on shelves spins poetry.

Fridge magnets plot a colorful dream,
A rogue banana teams with ice cream.
They murmur plans of night escapades,
While laundry waits in bright cascades.

Echoes of past parties blend with grace,
Nostalgia's a quirky, familiar face.
Silent witnesses of whimsies cast,
In quiet laughter, the shadows last.

Forgotten Corners of Existence

An empty box claims lost love notes,
Where hope once sailed on paper boats.
Forgotten crumbs hold a feast of cheer,
As dust bunnies lounge on the floor near.

Lemons lie low, a citrus scheme,
Squinting at life like a bittersweet dream.
Behind the couch, stories are spun,
Of pizza nights and sitcom fun.

The vacuum roars with a tale to tell,
Of marbles lost in a grand carousel.
A rubber duck smiles, so unaware,
Of all the drama that lurks in air.

Laughter lingers in every lost shoe,
A reminder of the joy that flew.
In each forgotten nook, a spark,
Where life plays hide and seek till dark.

Where Dust Bunnies Play

In twilight's glow, they spin and dance,
A party starts with just one glance.
Fluffy friends with no cares to share,
They laugh aloud, though none are there.

They race around, in leaps and hops,
Dodging crumbs and swirling mops.
With squeaks and giggles, they rejoice,
In their silent world, they have a voice.

The floor's their stage, they twirl and glide,
In this quiet haunt, they won't abide.
For every speck, there's fun at stake,
A dust bunny's joy is never fake.

So next time you see a fluffball fly,
Just know beneath it, dreams will lie.
Among the shadows, where no one roams,
The bunnies laugh and call it home.

The Unseen Observer's Gaze

With eyes of dust and frames of glee,
They watch the world so secretly.
From shelves of wood with stories grand,
In silence, they take their stand.

Not a soul knows they're there, you see,
Their chuckles float like a mystery.
Peeking out from books stacked high,
They wink and wave, but just pass by.

Oh, if the walls could only tell
The secrets they've seen, they'd know it well.
From spills of tea to whispered chats,
No awkward silence, no room for spats.

In every shadow, a thought unfurls,
These unseen watchers, oh what swirls!
With every glance that's cast their way,
They giggle soft, come what may.

A Lonely Chair's Confession

Oh dear old chair, with creaky voice,
You sit alone, not by your choice.
Waiting for someone to take a seat,
You sigh and dream of company sweet.

Each day you hope, with springs so tight,
For a little weight, to ease your plight.
You grumble gently, in perfect time,
With every chat, oh please, some rhyme!

"Here I am, all polished and bold,
With stories of laughter, both new and old.
Just take a rest, don't pass me by,
With comfy arms, let out a sigh."

But alas, again, the day drifts by,
You're left to ponder all alone, oh my!
Yet in your frame, there's love so rare,
A throne of whispers, this lonely chair.

Dust Motions of Memory

In swirls and whirls, they dance around,
Fleeting glimpses of years unbound.
Every flake holds tales untold,
Of laughter, tears, and moments bold.

Remember the party, the confetti fight?
When friends gathered close, in the soft twilight?
Now just shadows, with echoes of cheer,
Dust motes shimmer with ghosts so dear.

With every breeze, they spin and sway,
Recalling mischief from yesterday.
Beneath the light, they twirl in grace,
Reminders of joy in their dusty space.

So let them dance, the memories fly,
In the gentle hush, where time slips by.
Though days may fade, and moments tire,
In each little speck, old dreams conspire.

Unearthed Whispers

Dust bunnies plotting, schemes so grand,
A rogue sock leading a daring stand.
They whisper secrets, soft like a sigh,
In the shadows, where lost items lie.

The chair stumbles, a dance for one,
While a book complains it's never been spun.
The clock ticks laughter, a ticking tease,
Oh, the mischief in the forgotten breeze.

A shoe tells tales of wild adventures,
While the lamp hums softly, in funny ventures.
The dust settles in quirky ways,
With hints of laughter in these odd ballets.

On the floor, a crumpled note takes flight,
A grocery list from a tater fight.
With every twist of a distant sigh,
The room's antics make the hours fly.

The Hidden Interstice

In the gap where the light peeks through,
A cat is plotting, with an eye on you.
His whiskers twitch as he dreams of a snack,
While sock puppets ready a theatrical attack.

Between the cushions, treasures await,
Old popcorn kernels, a stick of fate.
The table wobbles, a dance of drama,
As the TV hums its quiet karma.

A note from last week's spaghetti night,
Whispers of sauce and culinary fight.
The dust motes tango in midair,
A silent party with laughter to spare.

Oh, the weirdness that takes its place,
With beetles in a congress race.
The wallpaper giggles at a feeble joke,
As the universe nods, with a friendly poke.

Soft Edges of Familiarity

Where the couch swallows keys without a care,
A remote is lost in a deep, plush lair.
The cat rolls in realms of cardboard and dust,
In this cozy kingdom, it's all a must.

In the light's gentle warmth, shadows collide,
Examining all the nonsense we hide.
A dusty old globe spins tales of yore,
Of silly places we never explored.

Oh, the cushions conspire in muffled tones,
As the rug dreams soft dreams of humorous loans.
Each forgotten item wears a quirky grin,
In this collage of joy, where silliness wins.

The laughter that lingers in corners and bends,
As the clock chimes softly, time never ends.
Nonsense abounds in every small space,
A whimsical dance, a gentle embrace.

Lines of Solace

In the lines of the walls where stories blend,
A quilt of odd memories starts to mend.
The chair has opinions; it creaks with sass,
While the dust collects tales of the daily pass.

A mischievous pen rolls under the table,
Waiting for paper to create a fable.
The rug whispers secrets of feet that tread,
Mapping the routes of the laughter spread.

Lights flicker like winks, oh so sly,
As the ceiling fans watch the antics fly.
In this snug little realm, hilarity grows,
With every odd object, a giggle flows.

The air is thick with memories and cheer,
In every crack, a chuckle appears.
The heart of the space, a smile's embrace,
Finding solace in this quirky place.

Inhabiting the Overlook

In a nook where shadows play,
A chair's always there to stay.
With crumbs from snacks that I have left,
It guards the secrets I've bereft.

A cat trots in with a curious glance,
Rights my wrongs with a little dance.
It peers at me, part judge, part friend,
In this funny place where moments blend.

Chasing dust that twirls in light,
I wave hello to ghosts of night.
They giggle soft, float away,
Mischief scattered in disarray.

Laughter bounces off the wall,
Here I sit, enjoying it all.
With a wink, the day draws near,
As I sip my drink without any fear.

Dim Light and Dust Motions

In dim light, where secrets dwell,
Dust bunnies tell their tales so well.
They jump and jive, no cares in sight,
In a hushed shindig, they take flight.

The old lamp flickers, winks at me,
A perfect host for my cup of tea.
As shadows stretch and bend around,
I chuckle quietly, no one is found.

The couch creaks with each little laugh,
As awkward gaffes make a funny half.
In whispers soft, the room conspires,
To turn my whispering thoughts to fires.

A sprightly dance with inanimate things,
In this realm, where laughter springs.
And when the day bids its goodbye,
I sigh with joy—oh me, oh my!

Corners of Contemplation

In corners, thoughts spiral like smoke,
Ideas collide, then laugh and choke.
With strange faces made of dust,
Conversations fuel this odd robust.

A thought bubble pops, it bloats and grins,
As my socks do battle, who'll win this spins?
The crumpled paper ball rolls nearby,
A reminder that humor can never die.

With sticky notes echoing past gags,
And half-empty mugs that smell like rags,
In silence, the playful echoes tease,
As dust swirls slowly, a gentle breeze.

I muse and ponder, lost in amusement,
In this cozy chaos of slight entombment.
Where laughter's a friend, never a foe,
In these bright corners, I tumble and flow.

Quietude Unraveled

In calmness found in cranny's embrace,
Dusty thrills find a cozy place.
With potted plants, all green and shy,
A playful whisper floats, oh my!

The tic-tac of a clock forgets,
Answering queries it never bets.
As I recline in cottony folds,
The space giggles while it beholds.

Jars of marbles roll and pop,
Imaginary games never stop.
I'm a king in this wild land,
With rubber ducks at my command.

A chuckle here, a snicker there,
Laughter bundles in the air.
All wrapped in quietude so mild,
In this wondrous kingdom, I'm just a child.

Forlorn Corners

In shadows gather socks unpaired,
A dancing dust bunny's lightly dared.
Lamp's glow paints walls with curious shapes,
While the cat's on guard, plotting escapes.

A plant whispers truths, or maybe lies,
As the clock ticks loud; time surely flies.
An old chair creaks, sharing secrets lost,
Of parties past, and the laughter tossed.

Beneath the table, crumbs pull their weight,
Rescue me please, I can't wait!
A ghost of pizza haunts the air,
The leftover slice, a foodie affair.

Quirky knick-knacks grin without a care,
Winking at me, they've stories to share.
A hidden world, where oddities dwell,
In lonely corners, all seem to gel.

Whims of Wandering Thoughts

A shoe's lost sole, on a mission to roam,
While thoughts like butterflies drift far from home.
Rebellion brews in the butter dish,
Dreams of becoming a gourmet dish!

The couch exclaims, 'What about me?'
It hosts many tales, oh, can't you see?
Why is there always a TV remote,
Lurking beneath like a secret boat?

It's a circus ride, this mind unchained,
Juggling ideas, all wildly trained.
One minute I'm off on a dragon's wing,
Next, a rubber band starts to sing!

With laughter bouncing off the walls so bright,
It's a party up here in the expanse of night.
When reason winks and chaos knows best,
Thoughts play tag; oh, what a jest!

Peripheries of Dreams

A boot with flair, and left all alone,
Claims the right to dream in monochrome.
Beside it, a shoelace, frayed but bold,
Entwines the tales of adventures untold.

In a forgotten sock, a world awaits,
Where penguins skate on icy plates.
Curious shadows dance on the ground,
Whispering tales of where fun is found.

A stuffed bear holds court with a rogue chair,
Hosting a tea party without a care.
Kettle sings softly, gurgles of tea,
As adventures bloomed, wild and free.

In corners unguarded, laughter will ring,
As memories echo, sweet little things.
An invitation to joy, tucked out of sight,
In stitched-together dreams that take flight.

Light Filtering Through

Sunbeams chase dust in playful delight,
As shadows flirt, turning darkness light.
An empty cup spins stories galore,
Of caffeine dreams and conversations bore.

A little mouse peeks from its cozy base,
Searching for crumbs in a warm embrace.
With each flicker of charm, it scoots about,
Living a life free from all doubt.

Ghosts of old recipes linger in air,
Spaghetti left-over whispers a dare.
While forks and spoons have a chat on the side,
About the best dish that they can't abide.

In this sunlit tableau, humor thrives,
Playing tag 'round life's cluttered archives.
Laughter breaks through like morning dew,
In a space where joy is always in view.

The Weight of Unspoken Words

In the silence, they all dance,
With silly steps, they take a chance.
Each glance a guess, a private game,
Who will speak first? Oh, what a shame.

Secrets float like dust in air,
I giggle softly, is it fair?
My lips are locked, they trap the glee,
Let's toast to words we'll never see.

Pillow fights of words unsaid,
I toss a laugh, like dreams in bed.
If only whispers had a sound,
We'd make a ruckus, laughter bound.

In this room, we're comedians,
Our jokes are trapped in truss of pen.
With every sigh, I feel the tease,
Oh, what a funny way to freeze.

Lurking Beneath the Surface

Beneath the couch, a creature hides,
Forgetting what the floor provides.
It's just a sock, but what a foe,
Ready to pounce, in silent show.

Crumbs gather like an audience,
Holding a strange, delicious stance.
Each one a tale, a bite of fun,
They giggle as I try to run.

Curtains wave with cheeky grace,
They know my every hiding place.
I swear they whisper, "Sneaky maneuvers,"
But I've got snacks, can't be the losers.

Daring shadows play their tricks,
I laugh and flinch, it's all a mix.
Beneath the surface, life is sweet,
Can't trap this humor in defeat.

Shadows That Remember

Oh look, the shadow on the wall,
Is that my dance? Or am I tall?
It waves at me in imitation,
A playful, cheeky interpretation.

They mimic thoughts that flit around,
In dim-lit corners, joy is found.
Each quirk and jig, a funny pose,
They know my past, but so it goes.

Every little laugh they've harbored,
Each silly moment we've not squandered.
Whispering tales, in twilight's glow,
Those playful forms, they steal the show.

In quiet spaces, life unfolds,
With shadows sharing laughter bold.
Together, we create the fun,
Their memory, my perfect pun.

Memories Clinging to Walls

The wallpaper holds my giggle fits,
And each crack tells of our silly skits.
Painted smiles hang in every hue,
With laughter splashed as colors do.

Nostalgia giggles in every spot,
A framed photo that hit the jackpot.
We posed like kings, but look at our hair,
Those taken moments, we can't compare.

Sticky notes scribbled with silly tales,
Each line like wind in joyous gales.
They flutter down like playful darts,
In this room of clutter, we sing our charts.

Memories cling with a form of grace,
Wrapped in laughter, they find their place.
I'll dance with ghosts of joy and cheer,
These wall-bound friends, forever near.

The Untold Stories of Shadows

In the light's retreat, shadows dance,
They whisper tales, given a chance.
A sock's lost mate, a forgotten book,
All gather 'round for a playful look.

The little dust bunnies hold a ball,
The chair creaks softly, like they're having a call.
A rubber band catapult flies with glee,
And even the broom joins the jubilee.

Under the Weight of Dust

A calendar hangs, months gone by,
Dust settles in without a sigh.
Old magazines hold secrets grand,
While crumbs form towns beneath the stand.

The vacuum cleaner's a beast on a roll,
It roams the floor, claiming its toll.
With each loud roar, the mice all flee,
The great dust debate — are we clean or free?

The Unraveled Threads

A ball of yarn goes on a spree,
Rolling and tumbling, oh so free.
Knots in the carpet wink at the cat,
As if they conspired with this and that.

Sweaters were once cozy, now in tatters,
While a sneaky ghost laughs — it's all that matters.
Unraveled tales twist under the bed,
Where stories of mischief and laughter are bred.

Where Solitude Sings

In the hush of dusk, a melody plays,
With footstep echoes, in quirky ways.
A misplaced shoe sings blues, oh dear,
While the lamp hums softly, "No one's near!"

The lonely clock ticks a playful tune,
And the curtains sway to a silent croon.
Every creak's a note, every shadow's a part,
Where laughter lingers and solitude's heart.

Beneath the Surface of Silence

In shadows lurk the dust bunnies,
A gathering of the lost spunnies.
They whisper tales of socks misplaced,
And giggle as the clutter's embraced.

The empty chair holds conversations,
With echoes of past celebrations.
Unseen friends share a joke or two,
While I pretend to join their crew.

A cobweb hangs with graceful flair,
A masterpiece in vacant air.
I chuckle at its grand design,
In silence, it draws the perfect line.

The clock ticks on, but who can tell?
Time's a jester, casting a spell.
Here, humor swims through quiet waves,
In this still space, laughter braves.

Threads of Abandonment

A lonely string hangs from the wall,
Once woven tales, now just a sprawl.
It flutters lightly, a tale untold,
Of mischief and laughter, bold yet old.

A shoe dangles high, a singular feat,
It once danced around, now admits defeat.
The laughter still echoes in empty halls,
A reminder of joy before silence calls.

Dust collects on an old board game,
Where champions rose and lost their fame.
Pieces are scattered, no one to play,
Yet memories linger, bright as day.

In this space, the fun's not lost,
For every cobweb has its cost.
A tingle of humor in quiet's embrace,
Where threads of abandonment find their grace.

In Subtle Absence

An empty mug sits by the door,
It once held coffee, laughs and more.
In its void, a joke takes flight,
A silent echo in the fading light.

A pillow sighs from lack of use,
Once a fortress, now it's loose.
It yearns for chatter, a pillow fight,
Yet sits in peace, a silent knight.

A tattered book lies on the shelf,
Its stories whisper of another self.
I crack a smile at chapters read,
In subtle absence, humor's fed.

With each pause, a thought will bloom,
In vacant space, there's still some room.
A chuckle lingers in every crack,
In subtle absence, we all look back.

The Art of Quiet Reflection

A mirror leans, a knowing stare,
Reflecting thoughts that linger, rare.
It holds no judgment, just a grin,
In its still gaze, the fun begins.

An unmade bed claims its defeat,
With pillows stacked, a loving seat.
It laughs at plans that fell apart,
Embracing chaos, an artful heart.

The light peeks in, a playful tease,
Dancing shadows escape with ease.
In the stillness, jokes slip by,
A silent comedy, oh so sly.

Beneath the quiet, laughter hides,
In every corner, joy abides.
The art of stillness holds a key,
To humor's dance, just you and me.

Where Sunlight Meets Dust

A sunbeam dances on the floor,
It tickles the dust, asks for more.
A lazy cat stretches in delight,
Chasing shadows, oh what a sight!

A forgotten sock is found again,
Worn out shoes that had their reign.
They share secrets of where they've been,
In a world where tales are spun thin.

The clock chimes loud, but who will care?
Time just laughs, like it's unaware.
As laughter bounces off the walls,
Faded echoes of long-lost calls.

So let us dance on this funny floor,
With dust bunnies spinning, we'll explore.
In this sunlight, we shrink and grow,
Embracing the oddities we know!

Solitary Whispers of Time

In silence, a sock speaks so clear,
Of a journey that brought it here.
It winks at the lamp that flickers bright,
As it dreams about the hugs goodnight.

The clock keeps ticking, but who's in charge?
A sneaky gnome or a paper marge?
Pens and papers make noises at night,
Swapping stories till the morning light.

A mug chuckles, it's empty once more,
Recalling the tea parties it bore.
Sugar cubes had their sweet fling,
Now all that's left is dust and spring.

Alone but together, these whispers fade,
In this quiet dance, a comical cascade.
Oh, the stories that linger on air,
In corners where secrets chuckle and share!

The Space Between Heartbeats

A fleeting thought flutters and sways,
Like a bird on a breeze with silly displays.
Tickles of laughter bounce in the air,
Hiding in silence, waiting to share.

The shadows play tricks on the wall,
Like a jester at a grand gala ball.
Echoes of giggles wrap around tight,
Spinning in circles, a joyful delight.

Between each tick, the heart beats loud,
While a chair creaks like a restless crowd.
Tales of old shoes and a missing sock,
An audience of dust, they all mock.

Yet in this space, where silliness reigns,
A lifestyle of laughter, joy without chains.
Catch the humor that fills the void,
In a world that's chaotically enjoyed!

Fragments of a Hidden World

Under the sunlight, they gather around,
Toys from the past, no longer bound.
A teddy bear giggles, a doll gives a wink,
In a realm where time takes a drink.

The sneakers plot mischief, the books roll their eyes,
As they hatch a scheme right under the skies.
Paper airplanes soar with a laugh,
In quiet corners, they play their own half.

A forgotten cap starts spinning tales,
About pirates and treasures and wind-filled sails.
In hushed whispers, they share wild dreams,
Of adventures that flow in moonlit streams.

So here they blend, these fragments so bold,
A microscopic circus, a sight to behold.
In whimsical harmony, they talk and they play,
Creating a world where we wish to stay!

Hidden Reflections

In shadows where laughter hides,
Dust bunnies dance, take their rides.
A sock lays lost, it seems quite grand,
Perhaps it's dreaming, a rockstar band.

A mirror with a smudge or two,
Looks back at me and laughs anew.
Who knew the wall could speak so clear?
It whispers secrets, just for my ear.

The lamp flickers, tells a joke,
Pretends it's shy, but then it pokes.
A forgotten vase, with flowers fake,
Smirks at me, for goodness' sake!

Oh, this place where nonsense rules,
Holds whimsical fables, like silly fools.
Behind each chair, a giggle stirs,
In this little nook, all seriousness blurs.

The Unseen Nook

Behind the couch, a treasure waits,
A half-eaten snack, oh what a fate!
There's a shoe that's lost its pair,
It dreams of dancing, unaware.

The cat's tail sways like a flag in play,
As if to say, 'Come join the fray!'
Ghosts of dust bunnies hop and race,
Creating chaos in this cozy space.

An old umbrella forgotten tight,
Claims to guard against a ghostly fright.
Yet all it knows are rainy days,
When sunshine simply went out to play.

Oh, laughter echoes from every nook,
In this silent tale, come take a look.
Each day a secret, whispering cheer,
In shadows here, there's nothing to fear.

Secrets of the Quiet

Whispers linger where dust motes dance,
In stillness, the frames take their chance.
An old dog snores, a soft lullaby,
While mischievous books ponder why.

Looking at me with knowing grins,
A coffee cup tells all of my sins.
Stale cookies gossip from the shelf,
'We may be tired, but still, we're stealth!'

The chair creaks jokes of long-lost tales,
Remembers when hostels had silky sails.
While posters giggle, their edges bend,
In this quiet zone, there's no end.

But here in this stillness, there's clarity found,
Where silently, joy makes its rounds.
With laughter and ease, secrets unfold,
In the softest whispers, life's stories told.

In the Stillness I Dwell

A spider spins threads of dreams so fine,
In shadows it hangs, sipping on time.
Tickle the silence, watch it jump,
As the corner blossoms with vibrant clump.

A pocket of giggles beneath the chair,
Where socks play hide and seek with flair.
The clock winks at me, what a cheek,
Sassily ticking, 'You'll never peak!'

Upon the shelf, things hold their breath,
As if to break out after their death.
An old bowl waves, a tale it tells,
Of countless snacks, its memory swells.

In this stillness, amusement brews,
With all these quirks that daily amuse.
So join the fun, take my cue,
In this quiet place, where laughter is due.

Silent Conversations

In the hush, the couch does creak,
A meeting spot for all that's weak.
Piles of laundry, a throne of fluff,
In this quiet chat, it's never enough.

The cat's judgment is crystal clear,
Staring at crumbs, he sneers with cheer.
Mismatched socks engage in a debate,
While dust bunnies plan a grand escape.

The clock ticks on with a lazy wink,
Rugged stains whisper, 'Let's not think.'
Chairs hum softly, a secret tune,
In this silent chat, who needs a moon?

Spilling tea on old magazines,
Gossip's rife among the machines.
With a wink, the table shares a joke,
While sticky notes laugh till they choke.

Where Dust Collects

The shelf stands tall with years of grime,
A monument to forgotten time.
Beneath the stacks of goofy hats,
Dust bunnies plot like sneaky rats.

Old trophies gleam with a ghostly flair,
Cheering for games no one would dare.
Do they hold secrets of lost finesse?
Or just remind us of our weirdness?

The vacuum rolls by, a clarion call,
Yet here they linger, wallflowers all.
Each crevice and cranny welcomes a giggle,
As they dodge the broom with a little wiggle.

In sunlight's spotlight, they perform their show,
Catching laughs in dust motes as they go.
They dance with the shadows, a comical flair,
In this haven of humor, with dust everywhere.

Fragments of the Unexplored

Beneath the bed, what treasures lie,
A world of socks and ancient pie?
The mystery calls, a playful tease,
As old leftovers fight for a breeze.

The closet whispers in worn-out shoes,
Echoes of laughter, they could amuse.
A tie from the '90s, a shirt with spots,
Fashion crimes shadow the overlooked thoughts.

Below the rug, a long-lost pin,
A battle with dust, who will win?
Each nook a chapter of silly untold,
In these fragments, the laughter unfolds.

Dreams and schemes hide in the seams,
Silently plotting their outlandish dreams.
They share their tales with a wink and a sway,
What hilarity waits in the clutter today!

Ghosts of Memory

An old chair rocks with tales to tell,
Of forgotten chats and a dinner bell.
It winks at the past with a nudge and a grin,
Whispers of laughter that bubble within.

The walls lean close, they know the score,
Echoing giggles from the days of yore.
Ghosts of spilled milk and cake gone wrong,
Taking center stage in a comical song.

The fridge hums softly, a respectful host,
To leftover pizza, we cherish the most.
Cartons half-full with a wink in the eye,
As they plot a heist with mischievous sighs.

In the corner, an old rug looks sly,
Its patterns could tell tales that reach for the sky.
Each ghost of memory a prankster, it seems,
With laughter that lingers beyond our dreams.

A Realm Beyond Sight

In shadows where the dust bunnies play,
I swear I saw my sock, just yesterday.
It winked at me with a cheeky grin,
Claiming its freedom, my laundry's sin.

That drawer of secrets, the sock monster's lair,
With mismatched pairs that float in midair.
I tiptoe close, heart racing with glee,
What treasures await? Just more laundry for me.

The ghosts of old toys, they gather around,
Conspiring to make all my snacks hit the ground.
A rubber band war against the cat's tail,
Oh, laugh if you must, it's a legendary fail!

In each crevice, a mystery to find,
Where all of my chaos is cleverly timed.
Embrace the absurd, let whimsy take flight,
In realms unseen, my heart feels so light.

Where Memories Linger

In a chair with a tear and a quirky lean,
A story's been born, but it's never seen.
It whispers of snacks and sitcom delight,
Of naps that extended well into the night.

Beneath the table, a long-lost remote,
Caught between crumbs and an old grape afloat.
Each click brings a memory, an echo of fun,
Like laughing at jokes told by squirrels on the run.

The wall's got a portrait with a crooked smile,
Of family vacations gone comically wild.
Each face is a riot, each pose a great feat,
A snapshot of joy in flip-flop and heat.

What tales these hushed spaces can share with a grin,
Of adventures so epic, they make the head spin.
So settle on down, let the laughter unfold,
Where memories linger, and life's never old.

Frayed Edges of Thought

My mind's like a sweater, all frayed at the seams,
With thoughts that unravel like wild, wacky dreams.
A stitch here and there, I patch up the gaps,
As I wander through theories, and goofy mishaps.

A notion once grand, now tangled and weak,
It flits like a butterfly—lost, so to speak.
Each idea, a puzzle with pieces astray,
I chase them like kittens that dart out to play.

Old socks as my muse, they take center stage,
Transforming my chaos, igniting a rage!
A ball of confusion, I juggle with pride,
In the circus of thought, I'll never subside.

So here's to the mess that's stuck in my brain,
Where laughter and nonsense are part of the gain.
Embrace all the frayed edges, the wild and the free,
In this colorful chaos, there's always just me.

Safe Havens of the Mind

In the attic of chuckles, where laughter runs wild,
My thoughts play hopscotch like a carefree child.
They twirl and they tumble, dodging the dust,
Creating a circus of giggles, a must.

A pirate ship sails on an imaginary stream,
Where rubber ducks sing and bubblegum dreams.
Here, seriousness fades like a shadow at noon,
As silliness blooms, to a jubilant tune.

Cartwheeling ideas on a trampoline high,
Bounce back with a wink, they'll never say die.
Each twinkling thought is an overly dressed clown,
Twirling in ruffles, never wearing a frown.

So welcome this haven, where whimsy takes flight,
In safe spaces built, everything feels right.
Let laughter be stitched through the fabric of time,
Where silliness reigns, and all thoughts can climb.

Faded Thoughts in a Quiet Nook

In a space where whispers cling,
Dust bunnies dance, doing their thing.
Forgotten socks hold a secret glee,
Awaiting their partner, oh where can they be?

A chair that squeaks with every shift,
Wonders if it's a ghost or just a gift.
The lamp flickers, like it's got a joke,
Making the shadows play and poke.

Old novels grin, their pages worn,
Sharing tales from dusk till dawn.
A teapot hums, with stories steeped,
While sleepy cats dream, undisturbed and deep.

So if you find a thought that's rare,
Take a seat and shed your care.
In faded corners where giggles loom,
Find joy in the quiet, in dusty rooms.

Veils of Light and Shadow

Sunbeams scatter across the floor,
Like silly dancers yearning for more.
Shadows debate on who's the best,
In their goofy game, they never rest.

A spider spins an intricate tale,
As crickets chirp, never to fail.
The cat in the sun, a royal pose,
Dreams of chasing a carrot that glows.

Chairs gossip in creaks and moans,
While the clock chuckles in tick-tock tones.
A rogue dust particle takes a dive,
In an epic quest to feel alive.

Here, laughter lingers in every beam,
In playful light, the shadows dream.
Underneath this comedic plight,
Joy wears a funny hat, just out of sight.

Tales Tucked Beneath the Floor

Beneath the boards, old tales reside,
Whispering secrets, side by side.
With every creak, a story unfolds,
Of mischievous mice and daring gold.

A sock brigade plans a great escape,
While dreaming of far-off lands and shape.
The floorboards chuckle with every step,
Their hidden humor, carefully kept.

The dust collects like forgotten cheer,
Sprinkling joy where no one peers.
An old potato, a hero now,
Stands mighty proud, but doesn't know how!

Every little scratch tells a jest,
In laughter's arms, we find our rest.
So tiptoe softly, take a chance,
Join in the tale, and laugh at the dance.

The Hidden Narrative of Space

In a world where the sofa's a throne,
Sits a curious cat, whispering alone.
Dust motes swirl, like confetti on cue,
As if the room's planning a party for two.

A coffee cup smirks, full of stories bold,
Of mornings missed and secrets told.
An old poster flaps, with a funky tune,
It knows the polka is coming in June.

The rug hums softly beneath your feet,
Hiding a dance from a past upbeat.
Imagine the old wallpaper's lore,
Every floral print sings of yore!

In a space that's alive, with laughter and play,
Every corner has something silly to say.
So linger awhile, let your heart be light,
In this hidden tale where shadows take flight.

The Edge of Perception

In shadows dance, the dust bunnies play,
With teasing whispers, they frolic away.
A sock rolls by, in a curious spree,
What secrets untold, do they hold for me?

A cat stretched wide, finds a sunlit throne,
Just watch her reign, she claims it alone.
The clock ticks loud, yet no one can hear,
Time like a tortoise, it just won't steer.

Chairs gossip softly, in creaks and in squeaks,
While curtains giggle, a secret that peaks.
Laughter erupts from the nearest old chair,
Who knew furniture had such flair?

Witty companions, this room's lively crew,
Movements unplanned, oh, who knew it's true!
In stillness they bloom, with antics unplanned,
Whispers of jest in a charming band.

Stillness Between Walls

The walls are blushing, they whisper and sigh,
As the picture frames watch, with a knowing eye.
A moth flits by, its wings all aflutter,
Is that a soft laugh, or just the old clutter?

In the quiet it chuckles, a flood of delight,
While the dust on the shelf plays its own little fight.
A spider spins tales in its silky, grand web,
Exciting the flies, all caught in the ebb.

Tucked under the rug, lost treasures do dream,
A paperclip couple makes plans on a beam.
They'll venture to fields where the lost items play,
As the broom rests too long, it's a dull, dreary day.

Yet laughter erupts, when the lightbulb winks bright,
And shadows break free, into soft, silly flight.
The stillness is golden, but with humor it sings,
Between these four walls, a riddle of things.

Rustling the Silence

Amidst the calm, a sock whispers in threat,
Should I chase that rogue, it's a personal bet.
The plant's placing bets on a dust cloud parade,
In this silent ruckus, adventures are made.

A chair lets out giggles, as visitors roam,
Their stories are woven in the fabric of home.
With pillows conspiring to create quite the scene,
Each wrinkle a giggle, each crinkle serene.

Books boast of journeys to lands unforeseen,
While crumbs on the table throw a delightful sheen.
Do they chatter in whispers, in pages unturned?
Or is it just me, with the humor I've earned?

With echoes of laughter, the stillness does shake,
Silly old shadows, for friendship's own sake.
Each rustle a punchline, each moment a jest,
In this blissful silence, we find our best.

The Overlooked Vantage

A view from the baseboard, oh what a sight,
Where dust bunnies gather, for laughter ignites.
The ants march in lines, oh what a parade,
They'll conquer the cookie, or so it's been said.

An old toy soldier keeps watch from a shelf,
He whispers to dust, 'Just be yourself!'
A vase tips with humor, a petal takes flight,
In this scenic chaos, all feelings feel right.

Curtains sway gently, like a dance at the ball,
While shadows embrace in a jubilant sprawl.
What wonders unfold in this whimsical haze,
As laughter and memories blink on in a daze.

So raise up your glasses, to moments we share,
In nooks and in crannies, with not a care.
Perched on this vantage, our smiles set free,
For the overlooked spots hold delightful esprit.

Places Where Time Pauses

In a nook where shadows play,
A clock forgot to tick away.
Dust bunnies laugh as they collide,
In this space, we just abide.

The cat naps on a sunlit mat,
While thoughts of dinner start to chat.
A teacup winks, a biscuit smiles,
Time's lost track of all its miles.

A sock is dancing on the floor,
Its partner's wedged behind the door.
Here, echoes know the quirks we hide,
Moments stretch with each wild ride.

Floating laughter fills the air,
As the couch becomes a throne to share.
Retreat from haste as life resumes,
In this realm where joy illumes.

Abandoned Dreams Reside

A kite hangs low, it yearns to fly,
But tangled up in a web of sighs.
Forgotten toys in dusty bins,
Whisper tales of failed spins.

A treehouse high, now fried by sun,
Where laughter danced and dreams would run.
The swing creaks softly, just for fun,
Echoing of days when joy was won.

In crumpled sheets of weathered notes,
Ideas float like worn-out boats.
They wave their hands, they shout a tune,
As the shadows sway beneath the moon.

Lost ambitions, they take a seat,
In a cozy chair that's bittersweet.
They sip on tea, with tales to share,
Of times when daring danced in air.

Within the Halos of Obscurity

A toaster hums a tune of grace,
While rubber bands throw a wild race.
Socks exchange a quiet glance,
As fridge magnets practice their dance.

A lightbulb flickers, feeling bold,
It dreams of shining, bright and gold.
But it trips on wires, falls to the floor,
And rolls away to tell one more.

Worn-out chairs with stories to tell,
Whisper secrets and half a spell.
Beneath the dust, a giggle hides,
In narrow paths where humor glides.

In shades of gray, the whimsy weaves,
Through crannies soft where laughter cleaves.
Surreal moments glide and sway,
In the gentle hush of a lazy day.

The Weight of Unsaid Words

A pillow holds the dreams we stash,
As silent whispers start to crash.
They tumble forth, a feathery flight,
In the stillness of the halcyon night.

Confessions dance in funny hats,
While socks form friends in chitter chats.
The coffee cup takes quite a stand,
As thoughts spill over, unplanned.

In jumbled piles, the truths stack tight,
While eyes roll back, avoiding the light.
Yet in the glances, humor gleams,
In the pauses that weave our dreams.

Crack the silence with a wink,
Let the laughter help us think.
For in the weight of what's unsaid,
Lies the joy that dances ahead.

Life's Quiet Witness

In the nook where dust bunnies play,
An old chair sighs in dismay,
With a creak it tells tales of the past,
Of kids, and snacks, and moments that last.

A lamp with a flicker, it often sings,
About wayward socks and random things,
It watches the awkward dance of the cat,
While pondering life and all of that.

Amidst the clutter and scattered cheese,
It rumbles soft laughter in the breeze,
Every trinket has secrets to share,
Even the broom has tales of despair.

So here's to the spot where silence reigns,
With a sprinkle of joy and small mundane gains,
Life's quiet witness, with humor entwined,
Finding the fun in the unrefined.

Whispers in the Shadows

In the shadows where the dust motes twirl,
A pair of old shoes begin to whirl,
They gossip about fashion from days gone by,
And the time that cat startled a butterfly.

A picture frame giggles without a sound,
Its edges frayed, its memories unbound,
It leans in close to the jar of coins,
Saying, 'Let's count the worlds you adjoin!'

Chairs hear secrets that walls hold tight,
The secrets of socks that vanished from sight,
A soft chuckle escapes from the rug,
As crumbs swarm around like a cheerful bug.

Every crevice bursts with tales untold,
A symphony of laughter in colors bold,
Where silent spectators guide the jest,
Whispers of the shadows, having the best.

Forgotten Spaces

In a room left to ponder and dwell,
Stale air is thick with an echoing yell,
A table leg wiggles, trying to dance,
As a wayward sock gets caught in a prance.

A closet sighs as it opens wide,
Revealing a jacket with nowhere to hide,
It chuckles softly at fashions once bold,
As moths weave stories in threads of old.

The ceiling spots waltz with the light,
Each shadow a dancer in shapes of delight,
A faint smile lingers on a painted wall,
As it listens to laughter's forgotten call.

Through forgotten spaces, whimsy takes flight,
In corners unseen, there's laughter in sight,
Boxes of memories and relics of fun,
Proclaiming the room is never quite done.

Echoes of Solitude

In solitude, echoes laugh at the air,
Where chairs sit idly, without a care,
A paperclip thinks it could be a star,
While a lonely old guitar mourns from afar.

The clock ticks in rhythm, a comedic beat,
With a tick-tock that dances on lonely feet,
It nudges the teapot, teasing a tune,
Whispering tales of a dysfunctional moon.

A rug hides marbles, a secret no more,
While cushions conspire on who should explore,
They swap tales of slippers that never returned,
And ponder the lessons that silence has turned.

Echoes of solitude, with humor heaped high,
In the spaces of laughter where we touch the sky,
These corners of silence, once serious, you see,
Are bursting with giggles, just waiting to be.

Whispers in the Shadows

In the nook where dust bunnies play,
A sock sneaks off, bright and gay.
Light flickers, the lamp's taking a nap,
Echoes of laughter, a lighthearted clap.

A cat leans back, plotting her heist,
While the rug rolls over, feeling enticed.
Old frames mumble secrets they know,
Even the curtains put on a show.

Crumbs from the cake hide under the chair,
The chair has a grudge; it's plotting, beware!
Tickles of dust dance through the air,
While a rogue spider claims the affair.

Oh, what tales these shadows might weave,
In this refuge where giggles believe.
A parade of oddities, it seems so clear,
Life is a jest when no one is near.

Secrets Gathered in Stillness

Beneath the table, a mystery brews,
A sandwich old, with curious hues.
The floorboards creak like an old man's cough,
While a coat hangs low, playing it soft.

A pair of shoes gossip, oh what a feat,
About the adventures of stray, happy feet.
A magic hat hides under the bed,
Pulling out socks that nobody's read.

Mismatched components, all have a tale,
A spoon and a fork? Ah, they never prevail.
A relic of laughter clings to the wall,
As the clock ticks by, no one hears its call.

In this silent realm where secrets hide,
Quirky companions take joy in their ride.
Spaces seem lively, as odd as they seem,
In the quiet of corners, we dare to dream.

Echoes of Forgotten Time

An empty chair hums a familiar tune,
Whispers of parties, now gone way too soon.
Cups on the shelf chuckle with glee,
From raucous to quiet—what kind of a spree?

Old photos grin, tales resting in frames,
Each smile conceals its own mixture of games.
The rug holds the memories of dancing shoes,
While a paper airplane negotiates views.

A feather floats down, tries to break free,
As the sunlight swirls through the old oak tree.
Tick-tock goes the clock, caught in a tease,
Magic of moments, stretched as they please.

Here's to the echoes of laughter and cheer,
In little spaces, our hearts find their sphere.
Forgettable times, forever divine,
In the stillness, no clock shall define.

Silence Stitched into Fabric

A quilt draped low, with patches of cheer,
Whispers of bedtime stories from years.
Buttons hide secrets, some good, some bland,
While stitches remember, both help and demand.

The bed springs giggle at tales they once bore,
Of pillow fights lost, laughter galore.
A blanket folds dreams, layered and warm,
Even shadows gather to witness the charm.

Old slippers shuffle, longing to sway,
As echoes of children come out to play.
A fabric of nostalgia, threads all around,
Weaving in moments we've cherished and found.

So here in this stillness, let laughter bloom,
In the heart of the silence, there's always room.
Lovely odd friendships, they snugly attach,
Dancing through fibers, unexpected to match.

www.ingramcontent.com/pod-product-compliance
Lightning Source LLC
Chambersburg PA
CBHW062112280426
43661CB00086B/496